#MeToo:

A Collection of True Story Crimes Against Women

Compiled by: Michelle C. Hillstrom

For all the victims and survivors. This is for you. You are not alone.

Table of Contents

FOREWORD

The stories and poems contained herein come from women across the world.

These women could be your mother, sister, daughter, grandmother, granddaughter, wife, girlfriend, best friend, coworker, boss, teacher, neighbor, or the woman you pass on the street.

These are true stories of crimes committed against women written in their own words. Some of these stores belong to the same women, meaning they had more than one story to tell, more than one experience.

I guarantee that at least one woman in your life has a similar story to these women. In my own case, almost every woman that I know has such a story.

This book was created out of my own need to tell my story. At least one of these stories belongs to me, personally. In writing my own story, I began to feel comfort, strength, forgiveness, and peace. I began to think that other women might benefit from writing and sharing their stories. That they might find some relief if they were able to anonymously share their stories with the world. And that those stories in turn might help other women know that they are not alone in their experiences and the feelings that come along with going through these kinds of traumatic events.

It is my wish that this book gives a voice to the women who have been silenced out of fear, shame, victim blaming, and the rampant rape culture and misogynistic culture in our society. That this book will help to change the stigma of shame that is associated with surviving these crimes. That it will give strength to the people who read this book, and that it will help continue the conversation of making changes to stop violence against women.

CONSENT REVOKED

I wanted to share my story in hopes it will save someone else from going through what I did.

I was a little sexually adventurous one summer, had multiple accounts on multiple different apps to meet new people. I got in touch with someone and asked him to come over. (We'll say his name is Sam).

Sam and I were hanging out and one thing led to another and we had consensual sex. I asked him to stay and hang out with me because I wanted to get to know him. As soon as we finished, he was a completely different person and left.

I saw him one time after that and that's when it happened. He raped me. After that, I didn't really know what happened.

"I invited him over. No, I didn't like it or want it but I invited him over, so it wasn't rape right?"

After that I got into a relationship with my now husband. When we had sex, it would trigger what happened with Sam. I would start crying and sometimes screaming. We couldn't have sex for months because every time we tried, it would make me cry. Even to this day, every once in a while, my husband will do something slightly different and it will trigger my rape.

I want to share so people know that even if you know the person or invite them over you can revoke your consent anytime.

UNABLE TO CONSENT

In 2005 I was just out of the Marines and living in my hometown, on my own in my first apartment. I dated a guy for about 2 months and then we broke up. I needed a relationship with sex he didn't want to have sex.

About 2 weeks later I was out drinking with some friends from work. One of the guys asked if I have ever tried a Xanax? I had not so he handed me the pill and I took it and drank for a for a while longer with them.

I woke up the next day not knowing what happened. I don't know how I got home, and my ex was in bed with me, and there were used condoms on the floor. I freaked out and yelled and screamed and kicked him out of the apartment. I called my best friend to talk to her and she said I had called her last night and I sounded really messed up. I looked through my phone calls and I had called most of my contacts.

To this day I still don't remember what happened and I am so mad at myself for putting myself in that situation.

THE BOYS

It was my junior year of high school. I got with a man that had already graduated. I was a virgin. One night we went to his friend's house and they were drinking. No big deal. But then they started taking pills. They wanted me to take them and they wanted me to have sex with his friend's girlfriend. I said no.

I don't remember much after that. I woke up in bed naked with my boyfriend, his friend, and his friend's girlfriend. I still remember nothing.

My boyfriend at the time told me I said "yes" later on. He said that he was my boyfriend, so it wasn't rape. Then I continued to have sex with him after that, because "I already had sex with him, so I couldn't say no now."

I eventually left him. I didn't tell anyone for 5 years. People still ask me why I didn't and don't report him. It's because I was scared. I was scared he was right. I was scared I'd be shamed. Then later on, I was scared I waited too long. No one would believe me.

Then I silently worked on myself. Now, I have fixed it myself. I have finally bounced back, and it doesn't hurt me anymore. If I were to turn around and speak out, I'd reverse all that work I put into my mental health. I can't do that. It doesn't hurt me anymore. But that doesn't mean it didn't happen or that it didn't count.

RETURN TO THE SCENE OF THE CRIME

Asphalt clicks under my wheels. My car pauses, lost in rounded hills that rise and fall, breasts of earth buried deep in topsoil.

The Palouse is a geographic anomaly. Ash from volcanic explosions seals the moisture into the thick layer of soil; a pastoral paradise of voluptuous hills crafted by a millennia of glacial silt into ideal farmland. This January, all is gray sky, white slope, black road snaking through.

The pond to my right is larger than I remember, but

smaller as well, wilder, a patch of urban wetland hidden behind the last row of houses, buried in leafy bushes. The hedgerow has become a jungle in the years since I've been here.

Pausing in the dark, pulling out my dead cellphone in a façade of security. Light shimmering on a blade a few feet away from me. My eyes adjusting to take in a large, long body looming just beyond the slim bodies of young trees where I stopped. Turning on my heels, shedding my flipflops, scarcely feeling the mud and grass as I raced to the house, knees pumping high as feet slapped on the ground behind me – reaching the front door, slamming it behind me. Shock, relief welling quaking through my body.

Waking up the next morning in a blanket of fear that would wrap round me for years, the tires of my cherry-colored Jeep Liberty ripped into ribbons in the parking lot.

My toddler grunts from his car seat in the back. I drive further into the wedge of hills, stopping at the square gravel lot behind the large barn, a landmark in the endless sea of hills. Iconic Americana.

My wee boy's little legs pump up and down as he runs up the path through the knife of cold air, charging to the wooden bridge, stomping across and back, leaning through to peer into the black water.

I want to linger in the moment, to sit by the trickle of dark water as my mind crosses by the someones who came here with me, swinging arms as we followed the asphalt paths into the pines and admired the pink mélange of the Japanese Magnolia. My eyes catch it from where we stand – the tree is a brown-hooded nobody in January.

Jack's brilliant orange puffer jacket sprints past, his strawberry blond curls rambling, his arms lifting to throw stones, in the water, dashes one way, then another. Laughing, yelling. Racing on.

BUT HE DIDN'T HIT ME

My most recent ex-boyfriend. I was in the Marine Corps. I met him while I was in MOS school. I had very little self-esteem stemming from my bio father and another ex..

This ex was a manipulator. He knew about my mental health. He knew about my anxiety and depression. He used it against me. I attempted suicide while I was in MOS school because of him. But thankfully, my mother called seconds before I did it. She could tell something was wrong and made me promise to go to the hospital in the morning. Then talked to me until I fell into a drunken sleep.

She saved my life.

But I stayed with him. That's what he did. He would break me down to my lowest then turn around and somehow make me believe he saved me. He did it for a year and a half.

We both got out and we lived together. I worked 3-4 jobs at a time while he stayed home. He would throw things at me, keep me awake fighting at night then get mad when I was too tired to go to work in the morning. He wouldn't work, clean, or care for our dogs. I basically starved myself to make sure he had food and I had enough money to feed my dogs and him and keep the WIFI on because he couldn't live without his Destiny.

He would sit on my chest, hold my arms down with his legs, and scream at me, poke me, and laugh at me while I cried and had an anxiety attack and couldn't breathe.

"But he didn't hit me."

He would shove me into walls and throw things at me.

"But he didn't hit me."

He wouldn't allow me to leave the house or room

he was in.

"But he didn't hit me."

He would smoke cigarettes and blow it in my face while forcing me to stay in the same room as him.

"But he didn't hit me."

The last straw was him coming at me in the kitchen and my dog shoving him back - trying to help me. He kicked her in the face. I attacked him. I punched him in the face. He told me that he'd really show me what being scared was like. Put me in a choke hold and I blacked out.

When I woke up. he was taking care of me. Apologizing. Blaming me. Blaming my dog.

"But he didn't hit me."

I finally left. I rehomed my dog because I she was too big to live in a semi-truck. She has a way better home now than I could ever have given her. She deserves the world for what she did for me. She saved me many times.

I told him I was going to go to trucking school and I'd drive a semi and make enough money that he wouldn't have to worry about working. Once I was in another state, I was still too scared to leave him. He would find me. He would hurt my family. I met a man that was helping me learn about driving a semi. I confided in him. He said he would protect me if I wanted him to. We could team drive together, and I wouldn't have to worry about my ex ever hurting me.

It's now been almost 3 years since then. I have a home, a career, and a man that loves me for me. That has helped build up my confidence to a point that I never thought possible. I don't want for anything. I am now a step mom of 2 girls and 1 boy. I love my babies more than anything and I couldn't imagine either of my girls ever feeling the way I did. So, I speak out.

DEAR SIR

Dear Sir,

You don't know me, but I was a first grader in the school that you were the principal for, back in 1999. It was an expensive private school, a K-8 school, one that was proud of its background. You probably forgot me, but I haven't forgotten my time there.

Your school changed me and not for the better. I started the year a happy little girl, a child who liked to play with Barbies and had a wild imagination. By the end of the year, I was someone else. I still had those traits, but I was no longer innocent. It was ripped away before I even know that the word meant.

Because I was molested several times that year by a middle school boy. Up to the point that I became *afraid* to go to school. Can you imagine? Children that young usually still enjoy school, but I used to *cry and beg* my parents with everything I had, *"please keep me home."* Because I knew what was waiting there.

You knew about this. It was brought to your attention. But you didn't want to do anything about it. I was shoved under the rug.

Let me tell you about my experience. The one I didn't ask for, the one you didn't want to know. You wanted silence, but now it's my time to dictate what is told.

It happened after school. My parents had to work, and I was in the after-school club. What should have been a happy time, became something horrible.

The boy-I didn't know his name- was also in that program. He would get me away from the group, in a small hallway away from the main one. I was too young and scared to know what was happening or to tell him to stop. I

23

knew it was wrong, even though I didn't have the vocabulary to explain why.

When he got me away from safety, he would take out his penis and masturbate as he stuck his hand between my legs and groped me, exploration that I did not want or ask for. Sometimes his hand went inside my underwear. The entire time, he loomed over me, bigger and stronger, as I was pinned against a wall.

These sessions were always quick, less than a minute or two. I believe if he had more time, he might have worked up to raping me. But he didn't have the time for that. At the end of each one, he always reminded me that I could not tell anyone.

These threats were so severe, so traumatizing, that all my small mind knew how to do, was shut down.

I became despondent, no longer wanting to go to school or play with my friends. In class, I would put my head down, not engage with the rest of the class. At home, no longer playing with my brothers. I took up a vow of silence, only speaking when spoken to.

This is how my family knew something was wrong.

Six-year-old children should not act like that. It took hours of my mother begging, pleading, crying for me to tell her what was wrong. His threat of *do not tell* terrified me, but finally, it all came out.

I didn't know what sex was, or even knew how to act sexy. I was too young. All the excuses that our culture makes, *"what was she wearing, how much did she have to drink, she must have led him on."* All wrong, I was a scared child. One that did nothing to deserve that pain.

This is where you entered the story. When I finally broke my silence, my parents, horrified, brought it first to my teachers and then to you. They wanted something done, they wanted action. After all this boy, he had to have been less than 14 years old. If a teenage boy that young was already laying hands on a six-year-old, what else had he been doing? How many others did he hurt? What kind of man did he become?

We'll never know. Because you said you didn't want that stain on your school, or for the news to get out. Nothing was done, he wasn't identified, or stopped. All my parents did was pull me and my brothers out and take us far away from the abuse we suffered at your hands.

I am an adult now, but what happened to me as a child still affects me. I have trouble trusting people, especially men. I dislike when strangers touch me casually, even on normal places like the shoulders or arm. I didn't date in high school and even now, struggle with relationships.

Once, a boyfriend had his hand on my knee and then suddenly moved north. On a knee-jerk reaction, I almost broke his nose. Because my body remembered. Therapy has helped, somewhat. I can talk about my story without crying, something I couldn't do earlier. But it still hurts. But how does one regain trust when they worry about who else might hurt you?

I do not blame you for that boy's actions. But I do blame you for your lack of action, for being complicit and turning a blind eye. Was I the only case, how many other children suffered under your leadership? *How dare you.* I was a little girl, trusted to your care. And you let me down. How *many others* did you let that happen to?

I hope we never meet again. Because I cannot make

promises for what I would and would not do.

THE FIANCÉ

I started dating someone who I thought was my soulmate. We dated for 2 years, then he proposed. I didn't realize it at the time but what he was doing to me was definitely not normal.

Sometimes when we were being intimate, he would cover my mouth and hold me down. I would cry and scream saying, "I don't want to do this." He never listened and just took what he wanted. Then he would apologize. I would be left feeling so hurt and confused.

After I finally left him, he would break into my house and do it again. Taking what he wanted and leave.

He said, "you are mine and this is my house. I can come and go as I please," even though he had his own place and a new girlfriend.

My family knew all about what he did. I said if they went to the police I would run away. I was brainwashed into thinking this man really loved me. Plus, I was molested by my step-dad as a child so I was scared and didn't have a backbone. When in reality, it wasn't okay.

I finally confronted my ex on what he did to me, after I left him. He had no remorse. I've ran into him once since I left him and moved. I get sick to my stomach every time I see him.

I used to be someone who always had a smile on my face. Someone who was always positive, and nothing could bring me down. Now I'm full of anxiety and depression. I've never spoken out to anyone else about this other than my family.

I hope this helps others share their story. I was blinded by what I thought was love, which instead was the nightmare of my life. I never thought I would be raped by my fiancé.

BODY ARMOR

I began to realize men solely saw me as their sex doll. I was raped on four separate occasions, coerced, manipulated, harassed, stalked, and assaulted.

They only wanted me for my body, so I made my body undesirable.

I gained eighty pounds.

Eating to comfort myself. Eating and building this fat body armor until there was nothing left of the "sexually desirable blonde-bombshell" with the "perfect body."

It was the only way I knew how to protect myself from their roaming eyes and groping hands. The only way I could feel safe. Safe behind layers of fat that shielded me from the eyes of men. Shielded me from their lust and desire.

No one looks at me anymore.

No one desires me anymore.

No one rapes me anymore.

I finally feel safe.

THE LANCE CORPORAL

I remember at boot camp during one of our school circles, the Drill Instructors essentially telling us not to get raped, but if we do get raped - not to ruin the guy's career over it. That stuck with me and it's what I was thinking about while I was being raped by a Marine that I met during MOS school.

"He's raping me. I'm being raped right now. The DIs told us not to get raped. I can't turn him in because it might ruin his career."

Completely brainwashed.

Here he was holding me down. Fucking me.

Violating my body. Telling me that I wanted this after I repeatedly told him that I didn't want to have sex, and I was worried about what would happen to him if I reported him.

I should have been worried about what would happen to me if I reported him.

Another Female Marine reported being raped by a different Marine a couple of weeks later. None of the junior Marines that were in our barracks believed her. I don't know if any of the Staff NCOs or Officers did. It did not appear that she had any help or support from them that I could tell. She was harassed, called a liar, and a lot worse. I don't know what happened. If he was ever punished. She and the male Marine were still there being held for all the processing when I finished my training.

I regret that at the time I was too messed up with my own stuff not to be able to step up and have her back. I regret that I wasn't in the right mindset to be able to report the Marine that raped me.

Telling my story now is the only way that I can think of to somehow do my part to help and make up for what happened in the past.

I thought Marines were supposed to be good and honorable. I admit I was naive. I thought they were supposed to have my back. That we were there for each other. That I could trust them. They were supposed to be my brothers, not my assailants.

IN THE BACK SEAT OF A CAR

I would drink. Much more than I should have and much too often. Even though I was a mother of three, I was only 23. I felt as though I had already given up too much of my youth, so I decided that drinking and partying was my way of taking back a part of that. My children would stay home with my husband (at the time), while I went out with my friends. This was an almost nightly occurrence. It is not a time in my life that I am proud of, but it has helped mold me into who I am today.

That night in March 2009 was no different than many nights prior. I went to my favorite bar. This time, I went alone. There were no friends to be met there, only drunken strangers. I became flirtatious with a man who I thought was attractive. We began talking and had several too many drinks together. I kissed this drunken stranger multiple times. As the flirtation continued, we decided to leave the bar together.

As this man walked me to my car, he began grabbing my butt. Though we had kissed, I was not comfortable with him touching me in this way. I playfully told him to stop. Nevertheless, I allowed him to continue walking me to my car. As we arrived at my car, I turned to face him. I was simply going to thank him for walking me to my car. He then pushed me against the car door and began kissing me fiercely. I put my hand on his chest, pushed him away, and told him I was done for the night and would be leaving now.

He then became angry and growled, "You're not going anywhere. I know what you want, you dirty whore." He forced me into the backseat of my car, with me struggling against him the whole time. Once he successfully wrangled me into the backseat, he locked the doors. One hand held me down by my throat as he fumbled with his jeans. In my drunken stupor, my strength left me. I could no longer struggle. I told myself that if I just let him do what he wanted then he would leave faster, and it would all be over in a few minutes. Inside my head, there was guttural screaming. Only heavy sobbing escaped my mouth.

As he began thrusting his pathetic manhood inside me, he began sucking on my neck. Hard. He told me he was going to leave marks all over my neck so that my husband would know what a slut he had married. When he wasn't biting my neck, he had his hand on my throat. When his mouth was on my neck, he pinned me down with his arms. I don't know how long the rape lasted. It felt like an eternity. He didn't use a condom and finished inside me. Once he was done taking what he wanted, he merrily got out of the car and wished me a goodnight. I said nothing and got dressed. I never saw him again. At least, I don't think I have.

I know this man's name. I do not remember his face. I resigned myself to never speaking of it. I resigned to pretending it never happened. When my husband saw the marks, all he saw was that I had cheated on him. I told him what happened. He replied by telling me, "Well what did you expect to happen? You were acting like you wanted him." I hid my shame in turtlenecks for weeks afterward. The bruises and hickeys felt like stains on my soul. After that, I didn't speak of it again until 2014, and only twice since then.

THE FATHER

When I was just 6, my father would take me in to the bathroom when my stepmother would go out to do errands. It started with touching. Then he had me perform sexual acts on him until he ejaculated. Then some days he would try to penetrate me until I was too loud because it hurt so he would stop. He would rub his penis on my privates until he ejaculated and made me lick it off of him. This went on for 3 years.

THE MANAGER

During the summer of 2003 HE raped me. HE and I were dating at the time. It was a relationship that grew from two years of flirting with each other at work.

HE was the assistant manager of the restaurant that I had begun working at my junior year of high school. It was a popular place for high school students to eat at and work at. Many of the employees were my friends from school. HE was a couple years older than me and we both had significant others over the two years that I worked there until I graduated from high school and had an ugly breakup with the guy who I had dated all my senior year.

Suddenly HE and I were both single and I was no longer in high school. Some places frown upon employees dating each other, especially when it comes to supervisors and subordinates, but if you have ever worked at a restaurant or a bar you know that everyone dates everyone. And our General Manager had dated and married one of the waitresses, so he didn't have a leg to stand on to tell us not to date.

Looking back now, I don't really know that you could really call what was going on between HE and I dating. He scheduled us so we almost always worked the same late-night shift together. I would stay and help him close. We would drive around a while afterwards sometimes end up at one of his friend's houses. The closest thing we ever did to actually going on a date was the night he raped me.

We went to his friend's graduation party. We got dressed up and rode in a limo to the party with his friends. Danced and ate and drank and had a great time.

When the party was over, we went back to his apartment where I had left my car. I went inside with him and sat down on his couch as I had done most nights of our short courtship. We started making out which I was fine with, but I had no intention of having sex with him. I was the kind of girl that would only consider sex if I was in a committed relationship and was in love with the guy. Neither of which was true about the situation with him.

I was drunk and my guard was down, otherwise I probably would have realized what was happening before it was too late for me to stop it. I tried to tell him no and to push him off me, but it didn't work, so I laid frozen with terror and disbelief beneath him until he climbed off of me and went to the bathroom to clean up. I no longer felt like myself as I stood and readjusted my underwear and dress. I no longer felt attached to my body. It was like my soul was hovering outside of me as I walked out the door of his apartment and got in my car. He didn't say a word to me when I left. He never called me again.

I don't remember many details from that night. It's been so long now and I blocked it out and pushed it down deep buried away.

I don't really remember how I managed to get

home. It's a miracle that I did though. My thoughts were jumbled and confused trying to process what had happened. Trying to figure out if it was rape. Rape was just something that happened to irresponsible women on Law & Order by random attackers and they were always beat up and bloody and bruised.

HE was someone I had known for two years. Someone I worked with every day. Someone who was friends with my friends. He was my boss. He was my kind-of-boyfriend.

I asked myself if it was really rape when I hadn't fought back, when he didn't beat me up. I had been making out with him and I wasn't a virgin and so… I decided that it wasn't rape, but that decision didn't help the hollowness that I felt within. The disgust. The sadness. The fear. The sense that my body was no longer my own. In a span of five minutes my life and I were forever changed.

I know now that it was rape. It took me years to understand and accept it. It was actually an article in Cosmopolitan that eventually truly helped me begin questioning and thinking about that night again.

But he knew that it was rape. HE made sure to cover his ass and make me look like the slut that wanted it from him. My first day back at the restaurant after the rape he had already told all the guys what had happened. His version of it anyway. Somehow during that shift, I was the only female working. The second worse day of my life. I was sexually harassed through the whole shift. He made it clear to all of the guys how badly I had wanted him and what a skank and freak I was. Sexual gestures were made with bananas. There was constant talk and laughing and whispering. I couldn't make myself small enough, invisible enough, or busy enough to avoid theirs leers, jeers, and taunts.

A job that I had once loved became something I hated. The restaurant was no longer a place where I felt safe. I quit a week later.

Rape is more than unwanted sex. Rape is about power and control.

It is mentally, physically, and emotionally traumatic.

His five minutes of pleasure took away everything I

was and everything I hoped to be.

All these years later, and I still think about it and relive it all the time. It is CONSTANTLY on my mind. I have nightmares about it. I still blame myself. I still wonder if I hadn't been drinking would it have happened? Should I have fought harder? I feel guilty for not reporting him because I'm scared that he did it to others too. Sometimes I think about reaching out to one of his other girlfriends that I know and am friends with on social media to ask her if he raped her too. I wonder if he regrets what he did when he sees my face and name on our mutual friends' social media posts and comments. I wonder what would have happened if I had reported him. Would have anyone even believed me? Or would the slut shaming and taunting only spread further into the community instead of just within the restaurant.

Would they have blamed me for what happened too? Ask me what I was wearing and how much I had drank. It seems so much of society immediately places the blame on women when they are raped instead of on the rapists. After all, even I blame myself.

EVERYTHING HAS CHANGED

Before I was raped, I was an extrovert.

I loved dancing, going to parties, hanging out with friends, meeting new people, being the center of attention, wearing clothes that complimented and showed off my athletic body. I had confidence and was full of life.

Now I can't stand to be around people for extended periods of time. I hide away, alone at my house. I hide my body under baggy clothes. I suffer from anxiety, depression, and have been hospitalized for suicide attempts. Even now, fifteen years later, I still struggle with confidence, self-worth, and trust. I struggle with trusting myself and my judgment, and I struggle with trusting men emotionally and physically.

I don't like to be touched or have my personal space invaded, which makes it difficult to be in crowded places. I don't like to sit with my back to a room. I always want to have my back to the wall.

Being raped completely changed my life and changed who I am as a person.

SMALL TOWN KIDS

This is a road I haven't gone down in a long time, and it's still pretty difficult. My #MeToo story starts when I was in High School when I was raped by 2 boys who I thought were my friends.

Small town kids look for any reason to party especially on a boring Christmas Break. This particular evening some band and football peeps were having a bonfire. I was a Junior and one of the only ones in my group of friends with a car, so I packed 4 or 5 people in the back and 2 in the front when it came time to head home. I made the rounds dropping people off at their respective places. I was absolutely in no condition to be driving. The last 2 people in my car were eighth grade boys. Their older cousins were in the band and on the football team so that's why they were there.

I remember feeling really drowsy at an intersection, and remember hearing the boy next to me say "You get out and get her, I'll put the car in park, then drive to our spot." I have no idea how much time passed, but when I woke up, my car was parked on a turn row in the middle of a field on the outside of town, and I was laid out in the back seat, clothes torn, bite marks on my breasts and what I learned later was semen all over my stomach and legs.

I got dressed and went home to my dad, told him what happened, and he took me to the hospital for an evaluation. We were basically told that small town politics would win out over any charges filed. The boys were from a well-known family in town, and it was suggested that we just forget it happened. Knowing I would have to go back to school after the break was over and face everyone who would no doubt know what happened, I wanted to quit school, and suicidal thoughts bombarded me. But between

49

my dad and my newly found church family, I stuck it out. It was a brutal return to school to say the least.

Then we go on to when I met my son's father. It was at a party with people I knew and 100% trusted, but he was there as a guest. I had a big drinking problem ever since my Junior year, and at this point I had just graduated High School. I vaguely remember being there, then the next thing I know, I'm home in bed waking up somewhere around 1pm.

A couple of weeks go by and I still talked to him and all of a sudden he busts out with, "You're pregnant."

Stunned I just look at him, "Uh, that takes a certain action to become pregnant, and I've not done said action with you."

He just grinned, "You don't remember? Too bad, it was kinda good."

And sure enough, I was pregnant. Flash forward through 8 months of being together and breaking up, my son is born and 2 months later his dad and I marry. Plenty of drunk rages and him taking what he wants by force during our 6 years of being married but hardly together.

One night in particular we were at one of his family members house for a BBQ. He gets wasted and I'm trying to take care of a 2-year-old and a drunk who is trying to show his family that I'm his and I do what he says. Except every time he tries that, I don't because I'm tending to our son, and therefore makes him an incompetent liar in front of his family who laugh at him for it.

That night after I put my son to bed, I think his dad is passed out in our bed. I start for the door so I could go to the bathroom, and suddenly he's up, out of the bed and behind me. He grabs me by my ponytail and slams me face first into the door and then down to the ground. He bound my hands behind my back with a shirt that was on the floor I think, and then he flips me over to my back. He apparently thought he turned into Rocky, because he used my face as a speed bag and proceeded to do other things as he wished.

My screams were finally heard by his aunt (who we were staying with at the time) and she came running in and had to kick him in the head to get him off of me. I don't remember if my son slept through it or not, but he had to be taken care of by his aunt for almost 3 whole days because my eyes were swollen shut.

To this day I can't have anyone standing behind me even if I know them and am comfortable with them. It sets off my Spidey Sense, so to speak.

HINDSIGHT

"(6) Rape is the penetration, no matter how slight, of the vagina or anus with any body part or object, or oral penetration by a sex organ of another person, without the consent of the victim."

I was raped.

This is the first time I am acknowledging that fact in words.

When it happened, I blamed myself. For leading him on, for being in his room, for being in his bed, for not consenting to do what he wanted me to.

I'll say that again. **I BLAMED MYSELF FOR NOT CONSENTING TO DO WHAT HE WANTED ME TO.**

So, he took what he wanted. He forced his penis into my anus and raped me.

I struggled, but he had waited until I was asleep and then held me down so he could do what he wanted to do. I made it clear this wasn't something I wanted. But he did it anyway.

The next day, I stayed in my dorm room, experiencing a pain like no other I had experienced. Pain, but also shame. I think I told my roommates, but I can't be sure. I didn't go to class. I had to sit on pillows.

But when he asked me out again, I said yes.

And I ended up in his bed again.

And it happened again.

And it was still rape.

I was raped twice.

By the same boy, the same way.

And although I was young and naive, and made some disastrously poor choices, no still means no.

I didn't see him again, and I tucked what happened

54

to me into the back corner of my mind, in the shadows of shame and regret.

I never considered it rape. I knew anyone listening to the story would say I asked for it.

Until #metoo.

Until women shared their stories, and I realized I had one of those, tucked in the back corner of my mind. And it was remarkably similar to others I had heard. And I began to test that word "rape" in my mouth. It felt foreign on my tongue, and given voice by my breath, but for the first time, I knew that word belonged to *me too*.

I remembered his name. Who could forget?

I looked him up.

It seems in the intervening years, he had a beautiful wedding. I saw video from it on YouTube. I saw his smiling face and thought, "That's the face of a rapist. He looks like any other nice guy on the street."

It seems he died young, maybe in a car accident? I'm not sure.

I wonder if he ever realized he was a rapist.

I wonder if there were others like me.

I wonder how the tendrils from this one secret, hidden in the back of my brain for all these years, have pushed their way into the relationships I've had.

I wonder where I go from here.

IT COULD NEVER HAPPEN TO ME

My time in the Marines was a good one. If I could do it all over again, I wouldn't change a thing.

People often hear about sexual assault in the military and may begin to assume that I am just another statistic to military sexual trauma, but that's not it. I am a mental health provider, a licensed social worker to be exact. I work with all populations and my last position was doing therapy with individuals who have experienced sexual assault.

I often thought to myself how something like that would never happen to me because well... I have all the training and am always careful. Not to brag, but I do my job well. However, I am human, and I see the best in people because I have seen just how resilient individuals can be.

Anyway, as I took on new position at a clinic, I begin to encounter new co-workers. In a short amount of time, I made some new friends that I was able to hang out with, especially since I am not from around here. My marriage of 8 years at the time was rocky... my husband and I were struggling, and he had moved out of our home, and my father's cancer was progressively getting worse. Before you know it, I fell into depression. I threw myself into my work and resorted to some unhealthy coping skills along the way (drinking to be exact).

I progressed well into my career and received a promotion; however, my marriage was falling apart and that's when he (the perpetrator) came into the picture. He was the clinic nurse manager and we got along well. I worked very closely with his boss (who is a good friend of mine); therefore, resulted in me spending more time with him as well. We worked together and eventually got to know each other on the personal level. We both had children the same age and found ourselves hanging out with other co-workers/friends more often (mostly drinking when we didn't have the kids).

Soon after that, it became birthday parties and park play dates. I thought we had established a good friendship and that's the only way I saw it. I didn't want anything more than a friendship and I made sure that was clear... and I thought he was clear too. One night when my children were with their father, I went to hang out with several friends including him. Once again, I began to overdrink. We went to several bars and then back to my house. He was just supposed to take me home. Several of us returned back to my house including him.

As time passed by everyone began to leave, I began to feel nauseous and needed to lay down. The rest was fuzzy, and I remember being uncomfortable and saying "no" and "stop" but couldn't move my body... I felt helpless and disgusted but couldn't move. I laid there and the unthinkable happened...

Was I just raped? Did someone I thought who was a friend just betray my trust? How am I supposed to tell my husband? The man who I was still in love with? The next morning, I felt sick and disgusted. The next couple of days felt weird to say the least. I went about my business and went to work. I could be over thinking it, but I felt like so many eyes were on me at work. I finally confronted him about the incident and in response I got, " you know you wanted it and liked it even though you said you didn't."

I couldn't even move after what he said. Was I just sexually assaulted? Did this really happen to me? This can't be happening to me! Not me! The professional therapist who is supposed to only help others. How can this happen to me? I thought about my husband and the pain I felt brought me to my knees. How am I supposed to tell him? I mean I knew we were separated but... how am I supposed to tell him? The worst way to tell someone something like that these days, I texted my husband and made him guess what happened because I couldn't even bring myself to say the words.

Over the next few months I struggled with my self-worth, had thoughts of suicide, and hit what you would call rock bottom. I knew I had to get help.

Finally, I did. I began seeing a psychiatrist and a therapist. Over the course of the next several months I worked on myself as a mother, friend, mental health professional, and daughter. I still have so much to work on, but I am one step closer to being the better me.

THE BROTHER

When I was in second grade, my grandfather passed away and that is when things changed. I remember getting home from school and doing homework with my brother. He wanted to show me something he found in dad's room, and it was porn. He wanted to watch it together and act some of it out.

He didn't rape me with himself, but with objects like pens, fingers, his mouth, and made me do things to him that a seven-year-old should know nothing about. I remember being super uncomfortable, but it was the first time he showed me nice attention, so I was very confused.

He told me not to tell mom and dad, or I would get in trouble too. This continued about once or twice a week until the age I turned 12.

I remember that night at my cousin's birthday party where we played truth or dare, and the question came up "What is your biggest secret?" I told her older cousin about mine and my brother's secret, and she went and told my aunt and uncle. They told my parents the next day, and my parents asked me about it. I told them everything even that they could find the porn in his VCR. I know they talked to my brother, but I don't remember much.

My mom told me that I was going to see the counselor that helped me when my grandad died, and I was excited. I was with my dad one day and I told him that mom was going to take me to a counselor for what my brother did. He abruptly said "I sure don't think that is going to happen," and it was never talked about again.

My brother became a drug addict and it brought a lot of hardships in my family. I forgave him because that is the kind of person I am, and I tried some synthetic marijuana with him during college. It took over my life for about three years, but no one knew. I could function in society, but it was killing me from the inside out. My friend took my keys away for a week and made me stay at her house to sober up, I will forever be thankful to her for saving my life.

Around the same time that happened, my brother relapsed and had moved back to mom and dad's house. We stayed up late to watch one of the Christmas shows we watched every year as a tradition, and my brother told me that he was sexually attracted to me, and he knew that wasn't right but really loved me in that way. He told me that his therapist said he became a drug addicted because he molested me.

I remember sitting there being so mad that he got to have an excuse for being a drug addict and I was just expected to be perfectly fine after he molested me so many times in my life.

I've never been to counseling, and I need to. Because of him my marriage is affected, because of him, I am on depression and anxiety medicine, because of him I don't enjoy sex and I have resentment towards my family. I know my dad didn't mean to hurt me, but I don't think he realizes how much pain it caused to feel like I was pushed to the side. My brother is selfish, and he has still never apologized to me, but I have found it in myself to forgive him and keep him in my life. Some day that could change, but I am taking it one day at a time.

Things in life happen, but you will be okay. It has helped knowing that so many other people have been through the same situation and stand tough. My molestation does not define me, and yours doesn't have to define you either. I am a strong woman, I am a teacher, I am a lover, and I am a fighter.

THE DAMAGED ONES

I grew up in a patriarchal household. I witnessed domestic violence. I was slapped around and had stuff thrown at me if I didn't obey the "man of the house." I've been told that my only worth as a woman is measured by how well I can care for my husband, both in the kitchen and in the bedroom. That my devotion for school and God were nonsense. That my pastor (who, growing up, was the closest thing I saw as a father) was only trying to take advantage of me because I was a naïve little girl who believed in a nonexistent God. All of this was done and said by the same man that molested me throughout my childhood: my mom's boyfriend.

Despite all of this, I still will never consider myself "damaged goods." I don't like the idea of being seen as a "good." A commodity. Something that could be bought, purely for another's enjoyment. A possession. And I don't want to be considered damaged. Damaged has so many negative connotations. Used. Broken. A waste of time.

I don't want to use my childhood as an excuse for all of my mistakes and regrets as a young adult. But the pain and darkness that I've carried because of my childhood, eventually became all-consuming to the point where I couldn't see anything past all the pain and darkness. In my childhood, he didn't just violate me once, he violated me multiple times. Physically, sexually, and emotionally.

I don't remember every single detail of what happened: when he first violated me, or even how old I was. All I remember are snippets: actions, words, emotions. I remember feeling scared, used, broken.

My cousins were hosting dinner one night. My mom was working that day, so her boyfriend, the father of my two younger siblings, was going to take us. That morning, he ordered me to grab my sister, take a bath, and get us ready to leave. Because my mom was away, I locked the door. Although my sister wanted to play in the bathtub, I wanted to hurry up because I didn't want to stay in the bathroom, naked, for too long.

Our doorknobs were the kind that if you were to undo a clothes hanger and poke it through the door, it would unlock. When I heard the lock on the door click, I remember my heart beating faster. I felt both scared and ashamed. This wasn't the first time he violated me, but it was the first time I was actually fully naked. I kept my head down as he made his way to the bathtub. As he grabbed the water bucket to pour water over me, I tried to hide myself from him. I remember he sent my sister away to get dressed. I don't think she even realized how messed up this situation was.

Wanting to get away from him, I got up to leave with her; however, he stopped me in time to shut and lock the door. Even to this day, it's hard for me to say what he did to me, because of how disgusting it made me felt. That day, he didn't rape me, in the sense of penetration. But he still raped me. All while it happened, I remember shutting my eyes, disconnecting from myself. My whole body just shut down, waiting for it to end. When it was finally done, he said the usual thing, "Don't tell your mom about this." He never had to threaten me, because I couldn't find it in myself to tell her.

With each time he abused me, I would slowly pull away from my mom because I was too scared of hurting her with the truth. I realize now that day, was when I lost my mom. My shame and guilt wouldn't let me face her after what he did to me.

There was another time when he came home in the middle of the day, while my mom was at work. He was out gambling with my uncles the night before. I remember watching TV while my little brother and sister were sleeping in the living room. As soon as I heard his truck pulling into the driveway, I immediately shut the TV off, scared of what he'd do if he found me the only one awake. As he walked into the house, I pretended to sleep while I clutched on to my little sister; she was like a barrier to keep him away from me. I remember feeling scared when I felt him standing over me, before hearing him walking towards the bathroom. Thinking back now, I think he knew I wasn't really asleep.

I don't remember if the phone rang for him or if he yelled out for me to bring him the phone. Either way, I think I did it because I was scared of him hitting me again, which were the consequences of me not listening to him. After handing him the phone, he blocked my exit and locked the door. I remember he was in nothing but a towel. He handed me a large wad of cash. His winnings from gambling the night before. He told me, "You can keep this money if you let me put this [points to himself] inside of that [points to me]." When I shook my head no, he told me, "Just this once, and then done. This will be the last time." *This will be the last time.* It's what he always said to me, so I wouldn't put up a hard fight against him.

But this time, I did fight. Next thing I knew, I was on my stomach, kicking away at him. Trying to squirm my way towards the door as he grabbed my foot, pulling me closer to him. I don't know if I started screaming for help, or if I yelled out my brother's and sister's name. All I remember is him pulling me closer to him. But I didn't stop kicking. I think at that point, he was scared of my siblings waking up, so he finally let me go. I remember he looked at me disgusted and as if I disappointed him: "You're selfish, I only asked for one thing!"

I was still really young at that time, and those words took away my ownership over myself and my body. It became difficult for me to tell the difference between something I actually wanted and something I *owed* to someone.

When I started high school, he slowly started to stop. But the damage was already done. By the time I was 14 or 15, I was recovering from an eating disorder and many suicide attempts. My relationship with my mom felt as if it was beyond repair. Even to this day, I sometimes find myself struggling to not give in to my suicidal thoughts.

When I was at Camp Johnson for PA School, I sought out professional help. That didn't last very long. It was maybe my 2nd or 3rd session with her; it was also my last session. Thinking back now, I don't think she even realized what she said to me, or the impact it had on me. It went along the lines of, "As a young child, being violated, you're introduced to different sensations. Sensations that you might have enjoyed, even while noticing that it was wrong."

I've relived those moments in the bathroom many times. I've remembered feeling scared, disgusted, ashamed. I've remembered wishing he would stop. I've remembered thinking about how I wanted to kill him. What I don't remember feeling was any sense of pleasure by that sick-fuck. Although I know it wasn't her intention, I was messed up from this. Even to this day, I'm scared of waking up from a dream of me *wanting* it to happen. I was plagued by thoughts of, "What if it was my fault?" What if I really did enjoy it?" Even though I can vividly remember hating everything he did to me, I was so scared of her being right.

Sometimes I wish I could have been stronger to protect myself against him. Other times I have an uncontrollable urge to kill him. He wasn't the only man to violate me throughout my life, but he was the first one who took away my voice and my right to consent or reject any sexual advances.

The thing that makes this worse is that I can never fully escape him because he is a part of my family. Before leaving for bootcamp, I told my mom that he's been abusing me. She believed me. She kicked him out of the house, but we never went to the police about it because I had to "think about my younger brother and sister." I feel as if I was stripped out of my own justice because of my "duty" to our family. He was the father of my two younger siblings (who still to this day, keep in touch with him). Even though his abuse happened over a decade ago, I have issues with connecting to a lot of my family members. Sometimes some of my aunties and uncles posts pictures with him on Facebook. Not everybody in my family knows what happened, but I feel disgusted and betrayed by those that do know and still treat him as family.

I try to avoid going home as much as possible. When I do go home, I prefer to stay with my husband's family. Other than my husband, he's the only one in his family who knows I was sexually abused. My husband and I have run into him a few times over the past couple of years. He hates him so much that even he wants to kill him. As for me, I always freeze. His face will always haunt me.

Today, I'm happily married to my high school sweetheart. He was the first person I ever told. Ever since then, he's supported me. I admit, I was really unstable when we first met, and we kept breaking up because of that. But during the times when we weren't together, he was still the person I'd call if I had a nightmare. I still have a lot of issues I'm working through because of what happened to me, but I'm trying to break the habit of using my abuse as an excuse for anything that goes wrong in my life.

Last I heard of him, he's supposedly dying. For the past year, he's been in and out of the hospital. When we heard about this, my husband laughed at his fate. "*Karma*," he says. Part of me is glad that he'll soon be gone. But another part of me somehow feels cheated out of this because he will die thinking that he didn't do anything wrong, because he *got away with it*.

Eventually I'll become more open and public about what he did to me, as a way to help other survivors as well.

But for now, I hope this written submission reaches out to others. Despite every negative thing that I've said in this submission, I want to believe that things will eventually get better. And to other survivors out there, I hope things eventually get better for you as well. We're not damaged goods. Our abusers are the damaged ones.

BROOKLYN NINE-NINE

My mom always led me to believe rape was a part of life. It seemed like no matter what I did, I would end up being raped. If you wear a short skirt. Rape. If you stay out past curfew. Rape. If you drink alcohol. Rape. For most of my life I just accepted its inevitability and almost wasn't even afraid of it.

I was almost 30 before it happened. It wasn't until even a year later that I even accepted IT for what IT really was. IT didn't fit the "definition". He didn't fit the "profile". IT couldn't have happened to me. If IT had happened, IT was my fault. So, I pushed that ominous 'R' word out of my mind. But it never really left my soul.

It was 2015, I was the happiest and healthiest mentally I had been in many years. I had a great job, my own home and was killing it at being a single mom. For the first time in years, I was single and so happy about it. I felt free and powerful. That all ended in one night. I was attending a party for a co-worker and a guy I had dated prior was there as well. We worked together, so I saw him frequently, but had ended our sexual relationship months before. I know better than to do shots of tequila because I never react well, but I ignored the voice of reason.

Earlier in the evening I had secured a ride home, but at some point in the evening they left and I stayed. I remember going to the party. I remember doing the shots. What I don't remember is what led up to the 5 minutes that would change me forever. Because I woke up in searing pain, dizzy and nauseous, my thighs burning and my cervix screaming in pain. I woke up having sex. I immediately knew where I was and who it was. But all I could say was, "STOP! STOP! IT HURTS!" He stopped and left the room. I crawled to the bathroom, threw up and passed out.

The next morning, I woke up on the bathroom floor to the sound of Brooklyn Nine-Nine in the other room. My heart hurt. My lower abdomen hurt. I couldn't find my underwear. He was asleep in the living room. I frantically but quietly searched for my keys and phone. They were where I usually left them when we dated months prior. I quietly left. I cried as soon as I got in the car. I felt sick. I hurt. Why is there dried blood on my thighs?

As I drove home, I called my best friend and ex-boyfriend to meet me at my house. I was in full blown panic as I got home. I hurt everywhere. I was dizzy and nauseous. My dress smelled like him. I threw it in the trash. I took the hottest bath my skin could tolerate. I sat there in shame. In shame and in fear. My friend told me to report it. To get a rape kit done and report it. I didn't want to. I didn't want to relive that moment for a doctor and a police officer. But more than anything I didn't want it to be true. Because after all I had known in my life, it was my fault. My actions led to a situation I put myself in. A situation, that if reported, could get me fired. We weren't supposed to date co-workers. I couldn't be unemployed. I have a son to think about.

I slept all day for 2 days. The pain wouldn't go away, so I went to the doctor for a pelvic exam. I never used the 'R' word. The bruising and the swelling went down, and an antibiotic was prescribed. I couldn't face HIM, so I acted cold and calloused at work. I felt to blame. So, I forced myself to forget. Weeks later I even apologized to him for being distant. It was my fault. Not his. We dated again months later. And we just forgot.

A year later, new job, new boyfriend and the weight of that night comes crashing down. Facebook memories pop up on my feed. A photo of that night. Me, in that dress. Sitting next to him. Right below it, a news article on my feed about Brock Turner. He looks like HIM. The same hair. I feel sick. I start thinking about that night. My friends at dinner in the photo. Doing shots. Waking up in pain. Where is my underwear?

I read the testimonial of the woman Brock Turner raped. That word. That four-letter word. Is that what happened to me? I didn't say NO. I couldn't. I was unconscious. Is it rape if we had sex months prior to the incident? I had stopped our sexual relationship and told him NO through texts for weeks leading up to the incident. I felt weak. Powerless. How could I let this happen? I started having nightmares remembering waking up in pain. The fear. The blood. Where is my underwear? I wet the bed. I woke up crying. I felt like a shell.

I told my boyfriend. He told me he would never have sex with me if I was passed out. In fact, the man I loved had slept next to me on the bathroom floor when I was too drunk to get in bed months before. He told me it wasn't my fault. He was mad. Not at me, but for me. I had been raped. The weight if that word was smothering. For weeks I could not breathe. I felt weak. I felt powerless. I couldn't even say NO. A choice was made for me.

It has been years since that night and yet it still haunts me. I wake up searching for my underwear, wondering why there is blood on my thighs, my body aching from a pain that will never heal. He stole something from me that night. My power to choose. Every year I think I am over it and those memories pop up on Facebook. That dinner, that dress, stupid Brooklyn Nine-Nine echoing through my head.

What he took I cannot get back. But what I can do is stop blaming myself. I am reclaiming my power.

WHY I NEVER CAME FORWARD

The guy who raped me when I was 18-years-old is well known to the majority of my Facebook friends. Well known to my circle back then. I could give details about him or name names and they all would know who I am talking about. And they would all probably be shocked. My Facebook friends would either believe me or not depending on how credible they view me as. I can guess who would believe me and who would call me a liar based on their responses to the rape trials that have been in the headlines. So many questioning what took people so long to come forward - calling people attention seekers or claiming it is all political moves.

But I'm not going to name names or give details because it would ruin his life. And it is a good life from what I've seen. Yes, I check up on him. Stalk him on social media. He is married. He is a father. He seems to be doing good for himself.

That is how fucked up and twisted my mind still is 16 years later. I can't ruin his life the way he ruined mine. I can't take away his future and everything good like he took away mine. I can't come forward because at this point, I can't prove that it happened. It would be his word against mine and all it would do is ruin his life and force me to relive it all over again. Cause me to be crucified. People would ask why I waited so long to come forward -just like they question the women in the news.

I'm only now able to accept what happened to me, for one. Even as he was in the act of raping me, I was in denial. On my way home that night I asked myself over and over "Was I just raped?"

I never told anyone when it happened. Let me repeat that. I never told ANYONE. Not my parents. Not my best friend. Not the police. Not a doctor. Not my psychiatrist. Because I couldn't accept it. Even though inside my soul was literally crushed and I felt dead. Even though I knew it was wrong. Even though I logically knew I was raped, I wouldn't allow myself to accept that reality. I wouldn't allow myself to say it because that would make it real and I couldn't come to terms with it. Even to this day I only confront what happened to me through writing.

I wanted to get justice back then, and still do to this day. I wanted him to know that what he did to me was wrong. I wanted to tell people and have someone pick me up off the floor and tell me they believed me and tell me I would be okay.

But he was well-known. He was well-liked. Everyone knew that I liked him. I didn't think anyone would believe me. I couldn't bring the shame upon myself and my family. I thought my parents would be disappointed in me. My rape wasn't like the rapes I saw on television. It wasn't violent. I didn't fight. I wasn't bruised and bleeding. I just froze. How would I prove I was raped? How could I go through a trial and be torn apart the way I saw them tear apart women on court shows? How could I ruin the life of someone I thought was a friend?

That's why I never came forward.

TRUST

When I was seventeen years old I trusted people easily, not like take candy from strangers or help an unknown person find their lost dog but I believed and trusted those in my life. I knew people could hurt you mentally, physically and emotionally as I had a very challenging family life, but I always wanted to see the best in people.

I was in a relationship with someone who at the time meant everything to me, we had been together for a few years and I thought we were happy until one day I found out he was cheating on me and it destroyed me, but the cheating was just the half of it. It turned out the person he cheated on me with was my very own cousin, I was angry, lost, sad and beyond hurt. Why would he do that? Wasn't I enough? Why her? I mean the questions were endless, but I would never find out the answer to any of those questions as that hurt and break in trust would be nothing in the scale of things.

I was heartbroken from my recent breakup and betrayal and I had this one friend who was funny, smart, older, and always knew how to help me take my mind off of things. We would go ice skating, dancing, roller skating, anything that was fun. He knew my family, knew my ex-boyfriend, and how sad and angry I was so when he invited me to go with him to get his car fixed, I didn't think twice. I mean why would I? We were friends, we hung out all the time, right? I can remember that day so clear as if It just happened yesterday and it was about 18 years ago. For all intents and purposes, we will call this friend Jack for jackass.

I had plans to meet Jack early one morning so we could go to get his car repaired, while they repaired it, we walked around, talked and had a great time as usual. Once they finished it was around lunch time, so we went to a nearby pizzeria and did what we did best laughed and laughed until my belly ached. Once we had finished eating, he spoke with another one of our friends and agreed that we would meet him at his job. When he asked if I would go with him to meet with our other friend I said yes, I was happy to see another friend, especially since I hadn't seen him in a few weeks.

We pulled up to our friend's job, he worked at a hotel as a maintenance worker where we had visited several times. We climbed out of the car and headed inside, it was so cold outside I was shivering when we made it inside. Once inside the building I didn't see our friend and when I turned my head to ask Jack where our friend was, I felt his hand grasp my hair firmly and I felt a shooting pain in my head. I immediately felt an unnatural amount of fear and when his second hand grabbed my neck and pushed me inside a room, I knew everything I believed, everything good was gone.

Jack slapped me in the face and said to not make a

sound, he once again grabbed my face with such a force I thought he would for sure pull out my hair. Jack said to stay quiet, to not make a sound or everything will get worse, I had tears streaming down my face and his face was blurry, but I could still make out enough to know that he looked angry, he looked vicious and I was scared. I tried to ask him what he was doing? Why he was doing this and every time I asked a question, he would grip me hard, pull my hair.

My heart was pounding so hard I thought it was going to come out of my chest, I felt like I couldn't get enough air in my lungs. He took off my clothes and I couldn't stop crying, saying no, please don't. He would just yank my hair, push or pull me to do whatever he wanted. He pulled us down to the bed and I just kept sobbing, trying to push him off but he wouldn't budge. I felt him climb on top of me and yanked my legs apart so rough I thought they would snap. I remember feeling like I was being torn apart, I felt such burning, I could feel him biting me, gripping me so hard I felt like I would bruise, and I kept telling myself to scream but I couldn't scream. It was like I was paralyzed from the fear that I just was there physically, and I could feel and see everything happening, but I couldn't actually do anything to react. I remember him saying how long he had wanted me, how long he waited, how patient he had been. He said I was perfect, I was a dream come true and all I felt was disgust, dirty, betrayal, angry, hurt and so many emotions.

He violated me so long and so hard I thought I would die right there, he kept confessing his love and all I could do was sob. Once he was done, he made me go shower with him where he proceeded to wash me and once again violate me. Once we were both showered and dressed he said we were leaving and to stay quiet and calm, I remember thinking how the hell was I going to keep calm when I was dying inside, my face was puffy and red from the crying, my head hurt so bad but I tried to calm down and I let him drive me home.

When we were pulling up to the house, he looked at me and asked if I wanted to go to the movies later that night? WHAT? Are you serious? He couldn't be serious, but he was. He truly wanted to take me to the movies, I said no that I needed to be home. He said he would call me later and I all but ran inside my house. I went straight into the shower where I turned the water as hot as I could take it and sat on the floor of the tub and sobbed, rocked back and forth and tried to process everything.

I don't remember how long I sat there, how long I cried but eventually I got up, soaped, and the water was cooler. Once I came out of the shower, I toweled off and looked in the mirror and could see where his teeth had been, and I could see where some bruising would appear. I took two Tylenols, powered off my cell phone, and laid in bed where I cried myself to sleep. I slept until the next day, when I woke up, I ached everywhere, I had a few bruises and bite marks noticeable, I was still puffy from crying and scared out of my mind. I kept replaying everything while thinking, did I fight back enough? Did I flirt with him? What did I do that made him think this was ok? How would I tell my family? Would they care? I decided that my family wouldn't care so I wouldn't tell them. I wouldn't tell anyone, I couldn't tell anyone. I went back to sleep, because while I slept I didn't think, I could pretend someone I trusted didn't hurt me, didn't betray me. My family never noticed all I was doing was sleeping, I avoided going out, I changed my phone number and I was in full blown denial.

Two weeks or so had passed and it was Valentine's day, the magical day of love and I was miserable, I was in full depression, I was still in denial and hadn't told a soul. Someone close to me begged me to get out of the house to go shopping for Valentine's day with her and so I finally gave in to stop being "such a downer" she shopped while I searched everyone's face because I was scared to run into "him".

After hours of shopping for her boyfriend, she said we needed to make a stop at the grocery store because she needed a pregnancy test, she said she felt pregnant and wanted to check because it would be the perfect present. She grabbed a box that had two tests and once we were back at my house she asked if I would take the test with her because she was nervous. I stupidly said yes and so we both took the pregnancy test, all I wanted to do was make her comfortable, make her feel at ease.

So, when we looked at both the test strips and hers

was negative and I had two very pink lines all I could do was sob and crumble to the floor. How accurate was this test? Why did I even take this damn test? Could I really be pregnant? Oh shit! Was I pregnant by my ex- boyfriend or my rapist Jack? Holy shit did he use a condom? Could I have a disease? NO!!! I refuse to believe this was happening on top of everything else. What was I going to do? How would I explain this? I was freaking seventeen-years-old. My friend was shocked I was pregnant as I was, so she ran back to the store and picked up four more test which all showed positive results. I was totally screwed and freaking out and still didn't know what to do.

I realized that I couldn't do this alone and I had to tell someone, so the next morning while my mom showered, I went into the bathroom and slid my hand carrying the test into the shower so that my mom could see it. I know it wasn't the best way to tell someone, I understand I probably could have handled it differently but at that time I couldn't look at her face, I couldn't see the disappointment. She opened the curtain, looked at my face and closed the curtain without a word. I was lost for words how do I tell my mom this? She looked so angry, but I had to tell her.

Once she was out of the shower, I told her to please listen to me and I proceeded to explain everything to her. She didn't ask any questions just said let's go. Where were we going? I didn't even dare ask because I knew better than to question my mother. When she pulled into the police station I was trembling, I was so scared. I didn't want to tell anyone else about what happened to me, but my mom said I had to tell them. I was taken to a room with dingy walls, a weird stale smell and the officer had his pen and notepad. He asked me what happened, so after a few attempts to speak and nothing came out I finally calmed myself enough to explain everything from who it was, when it happened, where it happened, how it occurred and everything that came after.

He looked at me while I was still crying and shaking and said he would be right back. He came back a few minutes later with a dictionary and pointed to the word "Rape" he said read the definition out loud. I was confused but did as he asked and read it out loud. He said if I was sure that I was raped and not crying rape because I got pregnant and got caught? He said that I probably consented and was crying rape. I remember crying harder and my mom just sitting there. I tried to tell him I was scared, confused and embarrassed so I didn't anyone. He said that without evidence, or bruises there was no report for him to take. He said that just because I had sex and didn't get a call back didn't mean I can make those kinds of accusations.

I got up on shaky legs and left, my mom followed behind quiet as usual, we got into the car and headed home in the most uncomfortable silence. Once we got home, I went and showered and went to sleep. The next day I went to the doctor's office as a walk-in to have the pregnancy confirmed and to figure out what I was going to do.

I was indeed pregnant confirmed by blood and sonogram, I was given my options of keeping the pregnancy, adoption, and abortion. I personally couldn't give my baby up for adoption or have an abortion. They also determined my estimated time of conception which was too close to both my ex-boyfriend and my rapist so I didn't know who the father was. The doctor explained that

I would have to wait until the baby is born for a DNA test unless I wanted to be tested while baby was still in my belly and explained the risk. I decided that I would wait until I had my baby and have the DNA tested with my ex-boyfriend.

I called my ex-boyfriend and explained to him in as little detail as possible what happened and that I was pregnant and he said that's good for you, I hope it hurt, that's what you get for breaking up with me. I couldn't believe it, I felt like I was drowning, and people were watching me but wouldn't help. I decided he and Jack could go to hell and I needed to figure out how to move on, how to push forward how to take lemons and make some damn lemonade. I told my family what happened, and no one reacted, no one cared, no one was angry for me. How could a family that should care about me not care, why can't I be loved? Was something wrong with me?

Nine months later and full-blown depression later, I had a beautiful baby girl who looked just like me. I was a mom and at that moment it didn't matter who her sperm donor was, I had enough love to give her, I would show her what real family was. I started reading self-help books and finding ways to deal with everything I was feeling. When my daughter was almost one-year-old I walked with some friends to the Chinese place up the block from where I lived and while my food was being made, I walked outside and came face to face with Jack.

He didn't live anywhere near me so I never thought I would see him again. I was frozen solid, I don't even think I blinked, and when he grabbed my arm and said, "Hi, I hear you had a daughter, is she mine?" I snapped out of my frozen place, yanked my arm and hauled ass. Chinese food forgotten, I ran full speed home, and locked my door. I grabbed my daughter and just hugged her while I cried, while I pleaded with the universe to help me.

I never saw him again, three years later I was finally ready to find out who fathered my daughter, so I went through the court system and was tested with my ex-boyfriend. Several excruciating weeks later the test came in via mail, and the fear at opening that later was horrible. It turned out that my ex was the father to my little girl and while I hated that, I was relieved that it wasn't my rapist. I moved from New York to Florida after that, I needed to close that chapter, I needed to not fear being outside.

I've worked really hard to put that time behind me, to not think about it, to not let it hold so much control over me. I still get nervous when I see a car that looked like his, I have a problem trusting people, I mean who wouldn't right? It's taken a long time, lots of hard work, tears, and growth, but I am in a better place.

When you are violated, it is unbearable and it changes you, but when it's someone you know and someone you trusted it's unimaginable and devastating. I know that what happened to me was not my fault, I didn't ask for it, and I sure as hell didn't deserve it. The only people who know what happened to me are my family members who still to this day don't acknowledge what happened to me, the police department that did nothing to help me, and about five people including the one person who gave me the courage and support to write this.

If something terrible happened to you it's okay to be angry, it's okay to be sad, it's okay to be depressed and untrusting, but whatever you do don't give up. You will not get over this overnight and everyone's journey is different. Get up every day and fight, live, survive. If something tragic happened to someone you love or know then support them, love them, help them. They may not ask for it, they may not even show they need you, but they need you more than you will ever know.

I'm a survivor.

WHAT BEING RAPED COST ME

I have spent almost two decades the repercussions of being raped. I was raped four different times by four different guys, and they were each someone I knew and thought I could trust.

What being raped cost me:

-My job that I enjoyed and had worked at for two years

-My freshman year of college and all the enjoyable aspects of being in college

-My Marine Corps Career

-The future that I had planned for myself before the

incidents

-My physical health

-My mental and emotional health

-My laughter

-My carefree happiness

-Friendships as I shut myself off from everyone

-My confidence

-My sense of security

-My trust in the people who are in my life

-Endless years of reliving the rapes over and over again

-Healthy relationships with men

-Every single thing that made me "Me" before the assaults.

Since my first rape, I have had a repetitive thought in my head. I wish that they had killed me instead. "I WISH THAT THEY HAD KILLED ME INSTEAD." Because at least then it would have just been done and over with. I wouldn't live with nightmares and PTSD and all the lifelong trauma that goes along with being raped. I wouldn't doubt myself, everything that I do, everything that I believe, and everyone that I allow into my life.

Being sexually assaulted IS THAT INVASIVE AND DEHUMANIZING. It's that violating. Like I said above, I've lost just about everything that made me who I was before the rapes. Everything about me is different. I even laugh different. It's basically like they killed me anyway. Now I often feel just like a shell of a human being. A zombie going through the motions, but not living. I am the Walking Dead.

CONSENT

We went on a date.

I didn't tell you no.

We drank a few beers.

I didn't tell you no.

We danced all night.

I didn't tell you no.

You drove us back to your place.

I didn't tell you no.

We were having so much fun.

I didn't tell you no.

We sat on the couch.

I didn't tell you no.

We began to make out.

I didn't tell you no.

You began to take off my clothes.

I didn't tell you no.

I tried to push you away.

I didn't tell you no.

You threw me down.

I didn't tell you no.

I tried to fight you off.

I didn't tell you no.

You were so much stronger than me.

I didn't tell you no.

I felt you inside me.

I didn't tell you no.

Everything inside me screamed no.

Still I didn't tell you no.

I went numb like a zombie.

I didn't tell you no.

I was no longer in my body.

I couldn't tell you no.

That body was no longer mine.

The body didn't tell you no.

I laid stiff as you finished.

I didn't tell you no.

You pulled yourself off me.

I didn't tell you no.

I laid there in shock.

I didn't tell you no.

I trusted you.

I didn't tell you no.

I straightened my clothes.

I didn't tell you no.

I walked to the door.

I didn't tell you no.

You didn't even glance my way.

I didn't tell you no.

I cried in my car.

I didn't tell you no.

Maybe I should have told you no.

Why didn't I tell you no?

I still blame myself.

I didn't tell you no. But I never said yes.

I never reported it.

I didn't tell you no.

How could I report it when I didn't say no?

I didn't tell you no. But I never said yes.

THE THINGS I NEVER GOT TO SAY

I hope that one day you read this and realize it's about you, and maybe you will finally understand that what you did was wrong.

I cared so much about you that I didn't even realize at the time what you had done to me qualified as rape. It took my friends to tell me. My therapist. Her husband (who runs a group therapy of sorts for perpetrators). Rape hotlines. And you. (Yes. You. You were the first person who told me that what I described to you was rape.) And it wasn't until you said the word "rape" that the pieces started to fall into place.

I finally understood why even though I wanted to be with you; I was afraid to see you and be alone with you. I dodged seeing you for a few weeks after the day you assaulted me, and I haven't seen you since. It took weeks for me to come to terms with the fact that what you did was sexual assault.

It's still hard to believe sometimes. I've pushed the emotional connection of it to the back of my mind so that it isn't the only thing I think about every day. Unfortunately, repressing that memory to some extent has left me with a thin emotional thread still to you.

Rape has always been one of my biggest fears in life, and I always believed that it was an incredibly violent act. However, my therapist (and many others) told me that most rapes aren't like what you see on TV where the victim is grabbed and violently raped in an alley behind a dumpster. Most rapes occur in situations like mine, and it's the grey line that now exists between what is consent and what isn't.

(In case you still aren't sure, what happened between us on your hallway floor was not consensual sex.)

I know you went through your own trauma that doesn't measure up to mine. At first you were furious when I brought it up, and you said that I was wrong. That's not rape feels like (because your assault was so much more horrific than mine). And I won't pretend like my story is as traumatizing as yours has been or compared to so many others. But I also refuse to bury my head in the sand and pretend it didn't happen.

You used to tell me that even with what you went through and while so many others have life worse - it shouldn't make how I feel any less valid. Until it came to what you did to me, and then suddenly you belittled everything I said and made me believe I was making it up for attention. And then you quickly went from blaming me to feeling bad. You said that if you had raped me, then you didn't deserve to live. You deserved to die a violent death and if you were like the monster who had raped you as a child then you couldn't live with yourself. With several suicide attempts already under your belt, I was guilted into staying silent.

But guess what? You panicked for a reason and went from angry, to feeling remorse, and finally back to anger. That reason is because you know deep down that what happened was wrong (in fact, if I remember correctly, when your new girlfriend called you out on it, you admitted and confessed to what happened and that you handled things horribly). But you blamed me because we were kissing and fooling around, and so I kept blaming myself and sticking up for you. It was my fault. I shouldn't have been playful with you. I shouldn't have had a pillow fight with you. I shouldn't have let you kiss me on the hallway floor, but it was fun and passionate.

Up until the moment I said no.

You kissed me and kept unbuttoning my jeans while I fought to keep them buttoned, pushing your hands away. Every time you would get the button and zipper undone, I would push your hands away again so that I could button them back up and zip them. You later blamed me because you said I must have forgotten the part where I had grabbed your dick, but the truth is that it was a distraction for me so that I could try to keep my pants on and get out from underneath you.

I remember telling you how much I hated the jeans I was wearing that day because they were stretchy jeans, and without a belt I felt like I kept having to pull them up.

You said you liked them because they were easy to pull off. And you tried. You kept trying. I told you I didn't want to have sex. I told you I was sore and wasn't in the mood, but you kept trying anyway. And when you finally got the jeans undone and down to my knees, you slid your fingers inside of my damp panties and murmured something along the lines of how it felt like I was in the mood.

Just because I was aroused and enjoyed kissing you doesn't mean I wanted to have sex. I still pushed your hands out of my underwear, but I was no match for you and after several attempts still trying to pull my pants up and keep them on - I finally stopped fighting. I gave in, and I hate myself for that. I wish I had been more adamant about saying a more forceful "no" or had pushed you completely off of me and gotten angry.

111

But I cared about you, and I believed that you cared about me, too. We had just discussed where our relationship could be heading, so I didn't want to ruin things with you. I didn't want to make you angry and lose everything we had and a future we could have had. I nonchalantly told myself that these things just happen. When you're with someone, you make sacrifices like this sometimes because it's what they want, and it will make them happy.

And so, despite the terror and dread that coursed through my veins, I finally gave in. I hated it. I just wanted it to be over, but I wanted to make you happy because I was afraid of losing you.

After that day, whenever you wanted to see me again, I felt sick to my stomach. I couldn't explain it at first. If I liked you so much and missed you, why did I feel too sick to drive to see you? It took time for me to realize that deep down I was afraid of you. When I said that I didn't want to have sex for a while, you said that it would be really hard having me around and not having sex.

It was that statement there that kept me up until 5

A.M. watching "Shameless" on Netflix. I was exhausted after work, yet I couldn't fall asleep. So, I watched episode after episode as your words swirled around in my head because deep down I knew that if you really wanted sex, I couldn't stop you. Even if I protested, I was afraid you would push your way in again.

I was falling in love with you, and so I knew that I would give in again. (People may judge me for that.)

Sometimes I wish I could go back and meet with you to talk about what happened, for I don't believe that what you did to me was done out of malice. It still doesn't make it right. I believe that if we had sat down and talked about it, then maybe you would have understood, and it never would have happened again. I truly believe that, and maybe that is why it has been easier for me to work on trying to forgive you.

But I never got that chance. You cut ties with me completely, and I found out that while I was still talking to you and helping pay for your therapy appointments - you were already on dating apps and had been out with other girls. It's how I learned you were lying about me the whole time. Here I was worried about you isolating yourself because all summer you only had me, and so I kept trying to insert myself into your life and be there for you. And then your girlfriend called for the truth.

She and I both realized you had been lying from the very first day you met her, and that you lied all about me and our relationship. Sure - we never had a label, but even she said we did have a relationship, and it wasn't as casual as you made it out to be. You never told her how I had been there to help you through the hard nights. How I answered every call and text, and how I was there when you would break down. You didn't tell her that I was the one who convinced you to go to therapy, and you refused unless I went with you. And I'm the one who told your girlfriend that yes - I had been in the room with you during therapy the first time because you begged me to tell the story of your own trauma.

After all of that and more lies were uncovered, I believe she still let you move in after knowing you for three months. Your therapist had said a relationship wasn't the best thing for you while you were healing, and I was patient and willing to wait to see what the future might hold for us. You didn't want me to leave either. But you jumped from crutch to crutch; I guess the few weeks without seeing me was too much for you to handle, and so you gave up on knowing me entirely.

I wonder today if you're seeing the same therapist, or if you are even in therapy at all. I wonder how you're doing, and I won't lie - I no longer wish you well. I still hope that one day you think back about how much I did for you. I hope you remember that I was the one person in your life that stayed no matter how much you tried to push me away because you didn't think anyone could handle your demons. You believed yourself to be unlovable, but I told you I would be different for you, and I would show you that were lovable. And I hope one day you reach out with an apology that would help me have closure because I've spent months talking to lawyers and the police, and I have been told that I probably would not win if I pressed any charges because I have no solid evidence. It was my word against yours. (Now I realize why so many survivors of abuse don't come forward.)

But I wanted to make sure that I researched all of my options, and it has been exhausting and tiresome. It has been emotionally grueling, but I wanted to try and be brave to pave a path for other women in similar situations. I want to be someone who can help if anyone comes to me with their own trauma. And I wanted to be heard. I wanted you to hear me. So while legally there isn't much I can do (other than the fact that your name is on file with the police department when I called in about a rape complaint), I wanted my story to be out there. In the beginning, I had read so many stories like mine, and it helped me to realize that what happened to me wasn't right. I wasn't alone. It helped me realize that even though my story wasn't one ripped from the headlines and making national news, it was still rape.

So I decided that I would write about my story. And perhaps this will be enough to help me begin to heal and let this (and you) go. Maybe this will help out someone else who reads my story (and oh I hope it does).

You had been unhappy all of your life. And you see - I had wanted to give you a chance at healing and happiness for once, but I didn't realize it would be at the cost of my own happiness.

ABOUT THE #METOO MOVEMENT

The 'Me Too' movement was founded in 2006 by Tarana Burke to help survivors of sexual violence, particularly Black women and girls, and other young women of color from low wealth communities, find pathways to healing. Ms. Burke, a social activist and community organizer, began using the phrase "Me Too" in 2006 on Myspace. Burke said she was inspired to use the phrase after being unable to respond to a 13-year-old girl who confided to her that she had been sexually assaulted. Burke said she later wished she had simply told the girl, "Me too".

Tarana Burke developed culturally-informed curriculum to discuss sexual violence within the Black community and in society at large. From the beginning, the vision for 'Me Too' was to address the need for resources for the survivors of sexual violence and to build a community of advocates.

The movement began to spread virally in October 2017, when actress Alyssa Milano used #metoo on Twitter and encouraged victims of sexual harassment to Tweet about it and "give people a sense of the magnitude of the problem" in an attempt to demonstrate the widespread prevalence of sexual assault and harassment, especially in the workplace.

In less than six months, because of the viral #metoo hashtag, a vital conversation about sexual violence has been thrust into the national dialogue in the United States. What started as a small local organization grew to a global community of survivors from all walks of life. The #metoo hashtag has helped to de-stigmatize the act of surviving by shining a light on the extent and impact of a sexual violence worldwide.

The original 'Me Too' organization continues to focus on helping those who need help with individual healing and by creating a community of survivors to disrupt the systems that allow for the global culture of sexual violence.

The goal of the 'Me Too' organization and movement is to reframe and expand the global conversation around sexual violence to speak to the needs of all survivors. Young people, queer, trans, and disabled folks, Black women and girls, and all communities of color. Along with wanting perpetrators to be held accountable, 'Me To' also wants strategies implemented to sustain long term, systemic change.

RAPE FACTS

According to the Center for Disease Control and Prevention:

 - Nearly 1 in 5 women (over 23 million) have experienced rape in their lifetime.

 - 1 in 71 men have experienced rape in their lifetime.

 - 13% of women and 6% of men have experienced sexual coercion in their lifetime.

 - 42.2% of female rape victims were first raped before age 18, with 29.9 percent of these from ages 11 to 17.

 - 11.8% of high school girls and 4.5% of high school boys reported being forced into sexual intercourse.

- Among female rape victims, perpetrators were composed of intimate partners (51.1%), family members (12.5%), acquaintances (40.8%) and strangers (13.8%).

- Among male rape victims, perpetrators were composed of acquaintances (52.4%) and strangers (15.1%).

- For female rape victims, an estimated 99.0% had only male perpetrators.

- 26.9% of American Indian/Alaska Natives, 22% of non-Hispanic blacks, 18.8% of non-Hispanic whites, 14.6% of Hispanics, and 35.5% of women of multiple races experienced an attempted or a completed rape at some time in their lives.

- 1.6% of non-Hispanic white men were raped during their lifetimes.

- Among sexual violence victims raped after the age of 18, 31.5% of women and 16.1% of men reported a physical injury as a result of a rape.

- 36.2% of injured female victims received medical treatment.

- Rape results in about 32,000 pregnancies each year.

DoSomething.org reports:

- Most college victims are assaulted by someone they know.

- 42% of college women who are raped tell no one about the assault.

- It is estimated that only 5% of sexual assaults on college campuses are reported, making sexual assault the most under-reported crime.

- 4 out of 5 rape victims subsequently suffer from chronic physical or psychological conditions.

- 2 out of 5 rape survivors develop sexually transmitted diseases as a result of sexual assault.

- Over a third of women who are raped as minors are also raped as adults.

- 42% of raped women expect to be raped again.

- Rape survivors are 13 times more likely to attempt suicide than are people who have not been victims of a crime.

As reported by the US Department of Justice:

- 62,939 cases of child sexual abuse were reported in 2012.

- In 2010, 12% of rapes and sexual assaults involved a weapon.

- Only 16% of all rapes were reported to law enforcement.

- In 2006 alone, 300,000 college women (5.2%) were raped.

- Among college women, about 12% of rapes were reported to law enforcement.

- In a 2012 maltreatment report, of the victims who were sexually abused, 26% were in the age group of 12–14 years and 34% were younger than 9 years.

- Approximately 1.8 million adolescents in the United States have been the victims of sexual assault.

- About 1 in 7 (13%) youth Internet users received unwanted sexual solicitations.

- 1 in 25 youths received an online sexual solicitation in which the solicitor tried to make offline contact.

- In more than one-quarter (27%) of incidents,

solicitors asked youths for sexual photographs of themselves.

- An estimated 60% of perpetrators of sexual abuse are known to the child but are not family members, e.g., family friends, babysitters, child care providers, neighbors.

- About 30% of perpetrators of child sexual abuse are family members.

- Only about 10% of perpetrators of child sexual abuse are strangers to the child.

- An estimated 23% of reported cases of child sexual abuse are perpetrated by individuals under the age of 18.

- There are 31 states that have no laws barring rapists from seeking custody or visitation rights, as reported by The Wire.

- Marital rape is "semi-legal" in 8 states, according to The Daily Beast.

- According to the Rape, Abuse, and Incest National Network, out of every 1000 rapes, 334 are reported to police, 63 reports lead to arrest, 13 cases are referred to prosecutors, 7 cases lead to a felony conviction, and only 6 rapists are incarcerated.

- They also reported that an American is sexually assaulted every two minutes.

Victims of Sexual Violence: Statistics

- On average, there are 321,500 victims (age 12 or older) of rape and sexual assault each year in the United States.

- Ages 12-34 are the highest risk years for rape and sexual assault.

- Those age 65 and older are 92% less likely than 12 - 24 year-olds to be a victim of rape or sexual assault, and 83% less likely than 25 - 49 year-olds.

- As of 1998, an estimated 17.7 million American women had been victims of attempted or completed rape.

- 82% of all juvenile victims are female. 90% of adult rape victims are female.

- Females ages 16-19 are 4 times more likely than the general population to be victims of rape, attempted rape, or sexual assault.

Women ages 18-24 who are college students are 3 times more likely than women in general to experience sexual violence. Females of the same age who are not enrolled in college are 4 times more likely.

- 21% of TGQN (transgender, genderqueer, nonconforming) college students have been sexually assaulted, compared to 18% of non-TGQN females, and 4% of non-TGQN males.

- 94% of women who are raped experience symptoms of post-traumatic stress disorder (PTSD) during the two weeks following the rape.

- 30% of women report symptoms of PTSD 9 months after the rape.

- 33% of women who are raped contemplate suicide.

- 13% of women who are raped attempt suicide.

- Approximately 70% of rape or sexual assault victims experience moderate to severe distress, a larger percentage than for any other violent crime.

- People who have been sexually assaulted are more likely to use drugs than the general public.

- 3.4 times more likely to use marijuana.

- 6 times more likely to use cocaine

- 10 times more likely to use other major drugs

- 38% of victims of sexual violence experience work or school problems, which can include significant problems with a boss, coworker, or peer.

- 37% experience family/friend problems, including getting into arguments more frequently than before, not feeling able to trust their family/friends, or not feeling as close to them as before the crime.

- 84% of survivors who were victimized by an intimate partner experience professional or emotional issues, including moderate to severe distress, or increased problems at work or school.

- 79% of survivors who were victimized by a family member, close friend or acquaintance experience professional or emotional issues, including moderate to severe distress, or increased problems at work or school.

- 67% of survivors who were victimized by a stranger experience professional or emotional issues, including moderate to severe distress, or increased problems at work or school.

- Studies suggest that the chance of getting pregnant from one-time, unprotected intercourse is between 3.1-5%[13], depending on a multitude of factors, including the time of month intercourse occurs, whether contraceptives are used, and the age of the female. The average number of rapes and sexual assaults against females of childbearing age is approximately 250,000. Thus, the number of children conceived from rape each year in the United States might range from 7,750—12,500. *This is a very general estimate, and the actual number may differ. This statistic presents information from a number of different studies. Further, this information may not take into account factors which increase or decrease the likelihood of pregnancy, including, but not limited to: impact of birth control or condom use at the time of attack or infertility. RAINN presents this data for educational purposes only, and strongly recommends using the citations to review sources for more information and detail.*

- An estimated 80,600 inmates each year experience sexual violence while in prison or jail.

- 60% of all sexual violence against inmates is perpetrated by jail or prison staff.

- More than 50% of the sexual contact between inmate and staff member—all of which is illegal— is nonconsensual.

- 14,900 military members experienced unwanted sexual contact in the fiscal year ending September 2016.

- 4.3% of active duty women and 0.6% of active duty men experienced unwanted sexual contact in fiscal year 2016.

- Of the 14,900 survivors, 43% of females and 17% of males reported.

Thank you for reading **#MeToo: A Collection of True Story Crimes Against Women**. Your purchase of this book will provide a donation to the Me Too Organization to help survivors of sexual assault.

Together, we can uplift and support each other and strengthen the global movement to interrupt sexual violence.

If you have a story you would like to share in #MeToo Volume 2 or #HimToo email me for information at mchillstromauthor@yahoo.com

HOTLINES FOR HELP

National Sexual Assault Support Hotline, 24 hours:

1-800-656-HOPE (4673)

National Suicide Prevention Hotline, 24 hours:

1-800-273-8255